We Can Reduce: Precycle It!

by **Sabbithry Persad**

Illustrated by
Jesse Schilperoort

ECOADVENTURES

An imprint of **Firewater Media Group**

Orlando

Several people have helped in vetting the content of this book. In particular, our sincere thanks go to Catherine Leighton (Program Manager, Waste-Free Lunch Challenge, Recycling Council of Ontario) for the expert advice and information.

Special thanks to Lindsay Schlegel and Mona Smith (editing), Joseph Gisini (cover layout), Jesse Cote (character design), Ravish Rawat (storyboard and draft illustrations) and Richard Barry (cover illustration).

Library and Archives Canada Cataloguing in Publication

Persad, Sabbithry, 1971-
We can reduce : precycle it! / by Sabbithry Persad ; illustrated
by Jesse Schilperoort.

(Garbology kids)
ISBN 978-0-9812439-2-4

I. Schilperoort, Jesse II. Title. III. Title: Precycle it!.
IV. Series: Garbology kids series

PS8631.E785W4 2013   jC813'.6   C2013-901333-4

Publisher's Cataloging-In-Publication Data (U.S.)
(Prepared by The Donohue Group, Inc.)

Persad, Sabbithry.
We can reduce : precycle it! / by Sabbithry Persad ; illustrated by Jesse Schilperoort.

p. : col. ill. ; cm. -- (Garbology kids)

Summary: After a trip to the landfill, Shamina and her friends decide to help reduce waste going
to the landfill by organizing a Clover Community Precycles It Challenge. In the process,
they learn how to reduce waste as well as help residents in Clover to reduce waste.
"Read - think - reduce."--P. 1 of cover.
Interest age level: 006-012.
ISBN: 978-0-9812439-2-4

1. Waste minimization--Juvenile literature. 2. Sanitary landfills--Juvenile literature.
3. Recycling (Waste, etc.)--Juvenile literature. 4. Waste minimization.
5. Sanitary landfills. 6. Recycling (Waste) I. Schilperoort, Jesse. II. Title.

TD793.9 .P472 2013
363.728

PERMANENT

We Can Reduce: Precycle It!

*For my parents Jean and Ramsaran ... and my siblings, nieces and nephews.
Thanks for the continued support.*

Shamina, Shakil and Adam climbed aboard the bus to sit beside their friends Tiana and Peter.

"I love school field trips," said Shamina.

"Me, too," said Tiana. "I'm glad the rain cleared. I'm excited about exploring the landfill."

"Especially after Mrs. Murphy's quiz...trash, garbage, rubbish, refuse, litter, offal...who knew waste had so many names," said Adam.

The bus left the school and drove through town, past the city limits. It pulled into a large landfill where garbage trucks offloaded waste into huge piles.

"Peeyoo, this landfill stinks," Shamina said, puzzled. "But the sign says Sanitary Landfill."

"Sanitary like protection from disease," replied Tiana. "This kind of landfill isolates waste, keeps it dry and prevents liquids from mixing with our natural environment. That way, odors, liquid and harmful gases aren't polluting our air, land and water as much."

"Which means it might have leaked today," Shakil said.

"That's right, Shakil, it's one reason why it needs environmental managers. But we're here today for another reason," said Mrs. Murphy. "Let's go meet Mr. Dinwiddy. He is expecting us."

Clover Sanitary Landfill Management Offices

Cell

Clay

Plastic Liner

Drainage Layer

Drainage Pipe

Gas Collectors

Material Waste

A landfill is carefully designed. It is like a bathtub in the ground.

"Hello, class," said Mr. Dinwiddy, the landfill's environmental manager. "Who knows what a landfill is?"

Shamina raised her hand. "It's a place where trash is collected and buried."

"That's correct. In Clover, we have a serious problem. Our landfill is filling up with too much trash. To solve it, we recommend cutting down on stuff we throw out each month. Who knows how we can do that?"

Landfill Types

1. Sanitary Landfill
2. Engineered Landfill
3. Secure Landfill

Landfills can be public (government-based) or privately owned.

"First we reuse, then we recycle," offered Peter.

"Super ideas," Mr. Dinwiddy agreed. "And before those, we can rethink our habits and reduce by consuming less. This is precycling—avoiding bringing home items that end up as trash or recyclable materials."

What is "precycle"?

"Pre-" means before, and "cycling" refers to recycling.

Together, "precycle" means *prevent waste before it happens* or *before you recycle.*

The word "precycle" focuses on reusing items, as well as reducing how much material needs to be recycled or thrown away.

What does it mean to consume less?

It means to buy less stuff or use fewer resources.

What is a habit?

It's a usual way of behaving. It's something that a person does often in a repeated way without thinking about it.

"Look at these bags," Mr. Dinwiddy said. "If pet owners chose large pet food bags instead of small ones, there'd be fewer bags in the landfill, right?"

"I get it," said Adam. "If I used a steel bottle for my drink instead of juice boxes or plastic water bottles, I'd avoid throwing out or recycling those items."

HAZARD ALERT!

Avoid throwing out items with chemicals or toxins that harm people, our planet and animal life. Your community may have special collections for those.

Ways to Precycle!
When shopping with your reusable bag, get things:
- in bulk quantity,
- that will have a long life,
- that are concentrated,
- with recycled content,
- with the least amount of packaging,
- made from materials you can recycle,
- that are not disposable,
- in reusable or returnable packaging.

"Most of the things we throw out is packaging," Tiana said. "If we carry reusable bags and choose items with no (or less) packaging, we can reduce the trash we produce."

"Absolutely. Precycling makes a huge difference in our community's future," Mr. Dinwiddy affirmed.

"Mr. Dinwiddy, if we precycle at home and at school, could our small changes reduce waste going to the landfill?" Shamina asked.

"Any small changes people make can have a great impact. And the more the community gets involved, the less trash goes to the landfill."

"I can see it now, Clover Community Precycles It!" Shamina laughed.

Before the class boarded the bus back to school, they sat down to eat.

"Hmmm." Shamina looked at her lunch. "We're using plastic bags and paper napkins. When we're done—"

"We'll throw them away," Adam finished.

"Right. If we think 'precycle,' we'd have reusable containers and cloth napkins," Shamina said.

Reduce lunch waste!

Pack a waste-free lunch!
Carry a "lunch precycle kit," containing a non-disposable container and silverware, cloth napkin and reusable bottle in a cloth bag that can double as a school bag.

That evening at dinner time Shamina and Shakil shared the class's trip and idea about the Clover Community Precycles It Challenge with their parents.

"We can start precycling now," Shamina said. "Let's use cloth napkins instead of paper napkins. The less paper we use, the less we'll throw out."

"I think a challenge is the perfect project for the Green Solutions Fair," said her mom, who was helping to plan the zero-waste event.

"Great idea, Mom!" said Shamina. "Then everyone in town can get involved. I'll talk about it with Mrs. Murphy tomorrow."

The next day at school, Shamina spoke to the class. "We can ask people to pledge to precycle. Then at the fair, Mr. Dinwiddy can announce how much waste the town diverted from the landfill."

"There isn't much time. Do you think we'll get enough pledges in just three weeks?" Tiana asked.

"Sure!" Shamina answered. "We started precycling at our house last night. Here's my lunch precycle kit instead of disposable packaging."

"I've got lots of toys that use batteries, like my video game console," Peter said. "I'll switch to rechargeable batteries."

Many of the other kids had already started precycling at home, too. The idea became so popular with the class, Mrs. Murphy assigned Shamina, Tiana, Shakil, Adam and Peter as coordinators of the community challenge.

During science period that afternoon, the group found some recycled paper and started making flyers.

Meanwhile, Mrs. Murphy contacted Mr. Dinwiddy to inform him that the group was coordinating the challenge.

Each Saturday before the fair, the group gathered at the community center to collect pledges. Many people hadn't heard the word "precycle" before, but everyone was enthusiastic about the idea of the challenge.

PRECYCLING:
HOW TO REDUCE

1. Avoid printing and switc to paperless billing

2. Purchase products in bu

3. Purchase products that are refillable or returnable

4. Purchase products with le packaging or reuse packagin

5. Purchase durable or reusa products, not disposable on

6. Use refurbished, recycle rebuilt or remanufactured pro

7. Rent, lease or share equipme

8. Use electronic tools like e-r e-books, e-music or e-newspa

PLEDGE

Back in class on Monday, they calculated the impact of the town's pledges to reduce waste going to the landfill.

But a week before the fair, they didn't have enough pledges to reach their goal.

That afternoon, Shakil, Shamina and Peter shared more precycling ideas before the fair. Tiana held a workshop and made a presentation. And Adam wrote letters to the local newspaper and organized a second-hand swap.

Finally, it was Saturday again—the day of the Green Solutions Fair. Everyone in town gathered at the park. Although there was a slow start, soon lots of people came to add their pledges.

The class finished their calculations just as Mayor Newton walked to the podium to address the crowd.

"Thank you, everyone, for your pledges. You have found many creative ways to reduce the waste our town produces. Thanks to Mr. Dinwiddy and Mrs. Murphy's class for teaching us about waste reduction and coordinating the Clover Community Precycles It Challenge."

Clover Community
Precycles It!
Population
100,000

Waste Generated
Per Person 4 lbs.

Waste Generated
Per Yr 73,000 tons

Waste Generated
Per Mth 6,200 tons

Waste Reduced Through Pledges
Per Mth 2,000 tons

GREEN SOLUTIONS FAIR

"Now let's see if we've reached our goal! It was a close call with last minute pledges, but in the end, we have pledged enough to reduce 2,000 tons of waste each month!" Everyone cheered. "That puts us ahead of our waste reduction goal!" The town burst into applause.

For the rest of the day, everyone celebrated their success, producing as little waste as possible.

Twenty-four years ago, one pound of aluminum made 21.75 12-ounce cans. By developing new technologies to reduce the can's weight, the can manufacturing industry now produces an average of 31.92 cans from every pound of aluminum.

According to the Environmental Protection Agency, American workers throw away enough paper every year to build a 12-foot-high wall from San Francisco to New York.

Since 1977, the weight of a two-liter plastic soft drink bottle has been reduced from 68 grams to 51 grams, keeping 250 million pounds of plastic per year out of the waste stream.

Containers and packaging represented about 28 percent of the materials source reduced in 2000, while nondurable goods (e.g., newspapers, clothing) represented 17 percent, durable goods (e.g., appliances, furniture, tires) 10 percent, and other solid waste (e.g., yard trimmings, food scraps) 45 percent.

For Reflection

1. Have you ever been to a landfill? If you have, what did you see there? If not, what would you expect to see?
2. What does "reduce" mean? What is "precycling"?
3. When we "reduce," "reuse" and "recycle" to protect our environment, which should come first, second and third? Why?
4. Do you have habits? Can you identify them?
5. How can you reduce at home? At school?
6. Discuss why it is important for the community to work together to address the landfill problem.
7. What is each person's responsibility to make a difference?

Why is reducing an important step before recycling?

The waste hierarchy classifies reduce, reuse, recycle and recovery in order of their environmental impact. Reduce comes before recycle because it prevents waste from the start. Cutting back on unnecessary things lessens the amount of recyclable materials you put in the recycle bin or waste materials you throw out as trash.

How can businesses help to reduce?

Along with precycling, businesses can practice source reduction—rethinking how they make and do things. Businesses can make efficient changes in product design, in manufacturing, in purchasing or with materials (the type and amount). Businesses can also avoid using toxic materials before they become waste.

Be an Environmental Manager

What is an Environmental Manager?

An environmental manager deals with all adverse effects of business and industrial operations on the environment. Typical day-to-day responsibilities include waste management, utilities conservation and legal compliance. Emerging legislation requires environmental managers to consider things like sustainable procurement, construction and environmental reporting.

An environmental manager must know how to reduce, reuse, recycle and conserve, and be able to develop ways to treat, use or dispose of waste.

Follow the steps below to investigate how your community can reduce.

1. Awareness of the Issues: Discover a *reduce* issue in your community. Analyze it to determine what makes it an issue. Identify different sides of the issue and the factors that affect it, such as personal values, business, the economy, cultural values and beliefs.

2. Investigation: Identify a *reduce* issue in your community and gather information about it using questionnaires, surveys, interviews and other techniques in order to understand all sides of the issue. Review the information and try to come up with two or three possible solutions.

3. Solutions: Brainstorm the solutions. Weigh them and select the course of action that seems most practical.

Experiments and Activities

Trash Math

Inspect (audit) how much trash your family generates in a given month.

Step 1 For one month, count how many bags of trash your family sends to the landfill. If you are not sure, ask your parents to estimate how many bags of trash your family produces each week.

Step 2 For the second month, apply ways to reduce the trash your family produces.

Step 3 When you reach the third month, count the amount of trash bags your family generates, then subtract the amount of trash generated in the third month from the amount of trash generated in the first month to see how much trash your family reduced.

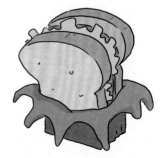

Auditing Your
Waste Materials

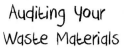

Reducing Your Trash
and Measuring Your
Progress

Reviewing Your
Waste Materials
Audit Findings

Reduce isn't just about minimizing! Look at the reduce symbol on this page. What do the three chasing arrows mean? For reduce to succeed, we must also work at conserving things. Look around your house or classroom and identify ways to reduce.

What else can you do to reduce? Start to use a reusable water bottle or a lunch box. Use the front and back of notebook papers. Perhaps you could think about the things you want and reduce it to the things that you need. Make a list of these and all your other ideas.

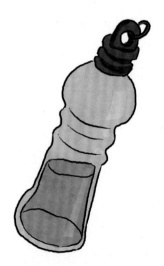

Note to Parents, Teachers and Librarians

Congratulations! Your child has taken the first step to learning about Environmental Science and Sustainability. The EcoAdventures® imprint is designed to introduce young readers to key concepts while challenging them to think about the world around them. Simultaneously, it augments their reading library with educational stories and books.

Read Think Do®

The EcoAdventures® set of books is a valuable addition to the home, classroom and library. Stories are designed to be read aloud to children, as well as to be read by a child independently. Images and definitions throughout the books are aids to learning the key concepts. The fun facts and practical lessons following each story stimulate children to think about the environment. Their understanding is strengthened by a hands-on project at the end. These books help children learn to question, analyze and interpret what they see; gain an understanding of environmental processes and systems; understand and address environmental issues; and learn about personal and civic responsibility.

EcoAdventures® Garbology Kids® Series

The EcoAdventures® Garbology Kids® Series uses humor to encourage greater learning and broader thinking about material waste, waste generation, waste management and waste technologies. It includes diagrams of the materials recycling loop and the waste management hierarchy. It also explains the most common principles of waste management, diversion and disposal: the chief Recycling Concepts (the 3 R's: Reduce, Reuse, Recycle), Transform, Treatment and Disposal.

Materials Reduce Loop

The symbol shows three chasing arrows. Each arrow represents a step in the reduce loop—auditing your waste materials; reviewing your waste materials audit findings; and reducing your trash and measuring your progress. When all three are done, we "close the reduce loop."

1. Auditing Your Waste Materials

Reduce your materials waste by monitoring your consumption and disposal. Be aware of what you buy and mindful of what you put in a waste bin.

Perform a waste audit:
a. Weigh your waste for a week.
b. Identify what you throw out.
c. Identify what you could avoid, reduce, reuse, recycle or compost.
d. Write down your results.

2. Reviewing Your Waste Materials Audit Findings

Review your results and make a plan to avoid, reduce, reuse, recycle or compost what you can for the short-term, mid-term and long-term, and start to make changes.

3. Reducing Your Trash and Measuring Your Progress

Now that you have a plan, you can start reducing! After you complete the plan and review your progress, set new goals!

Waste Management Hierarchy

The waste management hierarchy classifies waste management strategies according to the order of importance and desirability. Follow the Garbology Kids® Series to learn about each level of the waste management hierarchy.

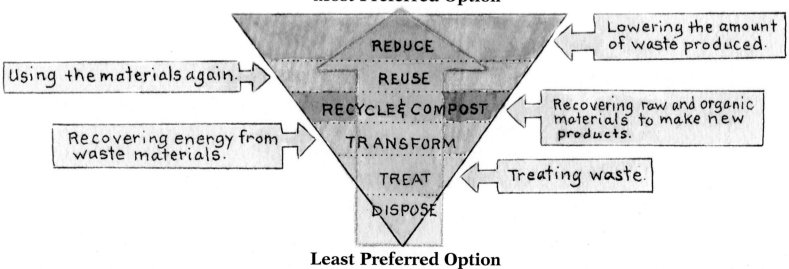

Most Preferred Option

REDUCE — Lowering the amount of waste produced.

REUSE — Using the materials again.

RECYCLE & COMPOST — Recovering raw and organic materials to make new products.

TRANSFORM — Recovering energy from waste materials.

TREAT — Treating waste.

DISPOSE

Least Preferred Option